With love to Spiro and Blossom

First published 1991
© Lesley Anne Ivory 1991

Design by Enid Fairhead FCSD

A CIP catalogue record for this book is available
from the British Library
ISBN 0 00 191392-1

Printed and bound in Great Britain by
BPCC Paulton Books Limited

CATS IN THE SUN

Lesley Anne Ivory

COLLINS

What a happy sight it is to see a cat enjoying sunshine. Cats adore sunshine and seek it everywhere. They appreciate the warmth left by the sun's rays on pebbled paths. They lie in pools of sunlight cast by the winter sun through windows on to rich carpets.

I seek cats wherever I go, and, like cats, I also seek warm sunny places, especially to enjoy holidays in, and never have difficulty in finding furry friends. I find them on quaysides watching fishing boats in little Greek harbours...

or by the side of small narrow streets feeding their kittens in sunny corners.

I love the way the sun shines through their ears making them look almost alight from within. And I love how the sun sometimes catches the outline of their fur and whiskers. If you look closely into cats' coats while they are basking in the sunshine, you can see many colours highlighted there, making each hair into a miniature rainbow.

They stretch and wash their faces on doorsteps, walls and windowsills, enjoying the first rays of the sun, or waiting patiently and hopefully for something interesting to come along. Cats have lots of time.

Butterflies are born into sunlight and fascinate cats who watch them fluttering about, and who then leap like ballet dancers, trying to catch them as they fly. Usually butterflies are just too elusive to be caught, but I have known my little Motley (herself a small tortoiseshell) successfully bring one down with her paws.

Cats use warm sunny days as an excuse to sprawl in your best flowers in the garden, preferably catmint which they adore, rolling over and spoiling the shape of the plant by quite flattening it as they writhe about on their shoulder blades, wild with joy at the fragrant smell of the crushed leaves and flowers.

In North Africa I found two nests of kittens outside one cafe.
One was in a hedge of hibiscus in full bloom, and when
I looked more closely the mother cat looked out and I could
see four little faces peering at me through the exotic flowers.
The other nest was in a tiled recess which had had geraniums
before the mother cat flattened them to furnish the "cot" for her
babies. I visited this cafe twice a day for a week, for coffee
and tea, but really to see how the kittens were getting on. The
owner of the cafe said, "You can have a kitten, no problem!"
"Oh yes, there is a problem," said my husband.
"She already has twelve at home!"

I have found cats sunbathing on famous sunwarmed mosaics, made by the Romans many years ago. I wonder how many cats have enjoyed the warmth of these little stones, and if they are even aware of the lovely intricate pictures and designs made of tiny pebbles, or the little squares of tesserae which made the floors of houses in days long past. Ancestral tigers and birds and fish and wonderful borders of patterns are now open to the sun, many bits missing through the ages.

Thousands of miles away in my garden at home, Malteazer is also enjoying the warmth of the sunshine, and rolling over on a mosaic I once made, using little fragments of broken china I found in ploughed fields. My mosaic will not last as long as the Roman ones. It is already cracking, but Malteazer does not mind.

We once shared a lovely picnic on the shore of a Greek island with a family of cats who kept fetching more and more of their relations when they found our picnic sufficiently tasty to be interesting.

Afterwards all but I fell asleep in the shade of a nearby olive tree.
I was looking at the interesting shells and stones and pieces of old pots
half sunken in the warm sand. Some hens and a magnificent cockerel
appeared and joined the cats to help clear up our crumbs, all among the
pink wild beach flowers and grasses.

At the end of the day when the sun is setting, cats may be seen making the most of the last little corners still in sunshine, washing their paws and faces, until the shadows lengthen, and the sun slopes round the other side of the world to awaken all the cats there.